My Fallen Love Language

Tariq Abdullatif

BookLeaf Publishing

Presentation by *BookLeaf Publishing*

Web: www.bookleafpub.com

E-mail: info@bookleafpub.com

ISBN: 9789357213875

First edition 2023

Dedicated to all those who are not afraid to love
and when they do, they love unconditionally
and courageously…

Just For Me

I know that you must be missing me, from the way that you are kissing me

I know that you're into me, it shows all in your chemistry

Don't give my blush away, I feel like you do it just for me

Flattered that you have a crush on me, and you can't get enough of me

Honored that you put your trust in me, and grateful that your love comes free

The thoughts of you alone can comfort me, you came and saved a wretch like me

You took the time to invest in me, in turn I became your property

I love you wholeheartedly , so much of you is apart of me

Yes I believe in your love, because I've felt it

I put my heart in your arms, and it melted

So much ecstasy in your air, I can smell it

You have me holding my breath, never exhaling

When it comes to pleasing me, you're excelling

And you're only playing the cards that you were dealt

God Has Blessed her, its only right that He test her

To see if she stands strong, or folds under pressure

She's exceptional, ring worthy, my treasure

She's always giving me more, then giving me extra

I pray The Lord rewards her for her efforts, and Bless her in all endeavors

A Sober You

I want you in sobriety
The real you
Not the person that you show to society
Bring your light to me, by being yourself
Indulge in yourself
While getting high off me
I want you to want me
Not because you were feeling nice
But because the feeling is right
Get full off me, empty me
Give me your energy
But first get back your energy
Put the bottle down
Give it a try with me
I want you complete
Be Free

About that time

As I look into your eyes, you can't even hide
what's on your mind

I would ask, what you trying to do, but i'm well
aware how you'd reply

We touched the sky, I touched your thigh, and I
got high

I didn't try, it slipped my mind, no parachute,
I'm about to fly

Turn around and let me take my time, as I
unwrap my prize

Gave you my heart and swallowed my pride,
told you I'd have to make you mine

I was walking around in disguise , but you seen
straight through my lies

You let me have my way with you, that was fine,
you subtly keep me in line

I'd gladly share what's mine with you, In fact I
want to share my life with you

Images of us in my head constantly on rewind

I cant lose you, so lets take things further

Its about that time

Alone

Adjusting to being by myself

I mean I'm comfortable, but I want to be
comforted

It's nice to take walks, but it's better while
holding someone's hand

What's the use of having this big ol bed , I have
no one to share it with

It's more than physical touch, hugs release
endorphins

Kissing releases stress

I have no outlets

Come home to space, and quiet

Peaceful, I can't deny it

But with no one to share your thoughts with

Silence becomes chaotic

Taking time to heal, they say it's part of the
process

I'm unsure of the progress, when constantly
feeling under duress

Believe in her love

Yes, I believe in her love, because i felt it
Her earth quaked, the ground split, and I fell in

I put my heart in her arms and then it melted

So much ecstasy in her air you can smell it
She has me holding my breath, never exhaling

God has blessed me with her, Its only right that
He me with test her
To see if I stand strong, or fold under pressure

I have no doubt, the reward is worth the effort
Because she's exceptional, a treasure

Can't Wait

I’m not trying to wait, I want you on my plate
I have an appetite for destruction, I just want a taste
Full figured caramel, my stomach growling
I’m warning now, I may bite off more than I can chew
I’ve been in line waiting patiently just to get a piece of you
Anticipation, I’m Thirsty, you’ll think I’m starving
Let me have it my way, please save the arguing
Panties fell like a rain drop
I’m sucking on you like a cough drop
Aint done till I make you pop
Or until I feel my heart stop
You all over me, but I’m on top
Skin on skin, but I got on socks
Tell me don’t stop and I can’t resist
Hard to fight the urge, but I must persist
If I had it my way, time wouldn’t exist
Caught up in our moment, love so intense
Staring in my eyes, you’re so intimate

Each position we choose so intricate
Wake up in the morning, when we come to sense

Looking at our mess, like how did we get into this?
Then you turn to me, with that look of sin
I invade your thighs, ready to dive back in

Conversate

Lets talk about it, can we conversate?
I know we standing on thin ice, and I'm not trying to skate
Seems like now a days you're easy to aggravate
I see the wounds still open don't want to agitate
All thoughts consumed with us, its hard to concentrate
My past is my past, one thing I can't escape
Yes I've been around the block, and you can't relate
I have to show you, you're my future and do what ever it takes
Words are just words, and everything aint what it appears to be
Its not always about what I'm saying, but my delivery
So what I have to do to keep you near to me?
A lot of things to me are dead, but not chivalry

Free Writing

They say adversity builds character, don't let
it capture you
Do what you have to do, to be a better you
We all striving to believe in what's actual,
but it's hard to leave doubts when they're
after you
Players get played too, and it'll humble you
When the one you ran away with, runs from you
Why chasing what we desire, always end in
heartache?

Because we're blind to fact, we don't control
our fate

We do control our actions, but can't control
the passion
Our hearts are blind, our eyes can see, our
brains get misdirected
We're drawn to who we think has all the
answers, but we ask the wrong questions
Because we only want to hear what we want to
hear, and not what we need to hear
Or rather we just want to do what we want to
do, and not what we need to do
We'll lay down before we do something that
makes us feel uncomfortable

We think the easy way is better, just give us the pleasure
But Adversity, it builds character, just don’t let it capture ya

Heartache

Heartache is physical
My pain is visual

Your love was conditional
Loving me in intervals

How do you feel it's permissible
To leave me here all miserable?

Now i'm feeling pitiful
For thinking that I could build with you

Still see your face in every female
Every dimple every detail

Always thought our love would prevail
But now i'm back on the market like retail
For resale

The other day i heard your voice in a sea shell
I guess i'm sick, Can't be well

Wish I had a preview
To show me how'd you act when I needed you

You're still flowing thru my system
Sometimes I drown just reminiscing

Toss and turn with every vision
Can't operate, you broke my piston

Your name still rolls off my tongue
When it does, I feel stunned

Your taste still spills from my lips
Can feel my hands still hug your hips
They miss the grip

I still feel the warmth of your breath
I'm going mad, trying to hold on to whats left

I just had to accept, there's nothing left

I need you

I need you
But I failed to show you that by the way that I
treated you

Sometimes I wish my heart was see through
So you could witness how I put everyone
beneath you

Still there's no excuse for what we do
Running around as if our feelings are not equal

I want to be the one to complete you
But you need proof
And you need truth
And me?
I just need you

I'd be lying

I'd be lying if I said I wasn't craving some
affection
Holding hands, exchanging hugs

I'll even settle for a long stare in my direction
To some this may sound depressing or desperate
I guess it's all about perspective
Who doesn't yearn love or romance?
It's refreshing!!!
Like breaking fast on a summer day
Can't wait till the thirst is gone
It's been too long, since I've had someone who
felt like home
Where I belong
Someone who feels like the lyrics to my favorite
song
I'd be lying if I said I don't mind being alone
I don't know how to handle it
What is life on your own?
What purpose does it serve?
I will admit that I've grown, and I had to do that
alone
Patient , Strong and a disciplined
I'd be lying if I said I wasn't ready for us

Is that Love?

Is that Love?
Treating you like a rug
Is that love?
Betraying your trust
Is that love?
When it gets physical
Is that love?
When he just spit at you
Is that love?
When you get ridiculed
Is that love?
When you feel pitiful
Is that love?
When you cant even talk
Is that love?
When you cant find the spark
Is that love?
Living in the dark
Is that love?
Weighing down on your heart

That's not love…love

It’s time to grow

Its time to grow

I never knew what I could pull, until there came the time to tow

Heavy my load, but still I wont let go

I was sprinting to my goals, but now I have to take it slow

Different approach, in time I’m going to blow

Practice patience with my hopes, and never let my worries show

Only in God, I will consult, His worship is what I owe

It’s hard to keep your spirits high when your faith drags down below

Next stop is transformation, it’s time to glow

Whenever my past come around, it’s time to go

I’m being stingy with my energy and my feelings are on hold

Please don't take it personal

It’s just that it’s time to grow, Lord knows it’s time to grow

Lessons Learned

You play with fire you get burned
And we'll call that a lesson learned
When it's your turn. It's your turn
Seize the opportunity when it appears
Take what you can while its there
Dont put off tomorrow, what you can do today
Words can hurt more than fist
If they showed you who they are, believe them
The loudest in the room is the weakest
Shy guys finish last
Be humble, dont brag
You cant predict the weather
God is the Controller of all affairs
You cant question God
You aint a boss, if you cant take a loss
Mercy aint a sign of weakness, its a sign of
strength
Men do what they have to do, boys do what they
want
Adversity doesnt build character, it reveals
character
Being dumb isnt saying that you do not know
Being dumb is saying you know, when you don't
All money isnt good money
Slow money better than no money
Its not what you have, its what you keep

Prayer is better than sleep
One who keeps his own secrets controls his own affairs
Judge a man's intelligence, by the questions he ask
Experience is knowledge gained
Self reflection brings self correction
Believe nothing you hear, half of what you see

Love is

Love is laughing
Love is smiling
Love is having your number memorized while
I'm dialing
Love is seeing your face
Love is invading your space
Love is our first kiss
Love is our first argument
Love is making up, and getting over it
Love is you on my mind
Love is intoxicating like wine
Love is chills down your spine
Love is me taking my time
Love is lifting you up
Love is helping you grow
Love is a feeling in your gut
When you know, you just know
Not hungry, but thirsty for you
Love is you quenching my thirst
You're not a snack, you're a meal
You're not a deal, you're a steal
I'm thankful for you
I'm just keeping it real
Love is a 30 minute clip
Love is a 45 minute wait

Love is a 3 and a half hour drive, for only an
hour in your face
Love is i'll see you another day
Love is holding you in my embrace
Love is missing you along the way, as I walk
back into this empty place
Love is watermelon sour patch
Love is the color red
Love is that hijab upon your head
Love is your favorite book
Love is after a long day, the comfort of your bed
Love is Patience
Love is the climax without the sex
There is no love without respect
Love is Integrity
Love is you questioning me
Love is consoling
Love is being content
Love is relentless
Love is Free

Matter of Time

It's no mirage
Everytime I think about us
I see us together like a collage
Just a matter of time

I like the questions you ask
I like that you want to know
You have my attention in your grasp
I like how you demand control
You wont settle for last
You know exactly where you want to go

I want to lose myself in you
To the point that I say what's on your mind
I'm tryna find my way to your heart
Just a matter of time

I know you wonder how can I be so sure
Certain that you're everything I want and more
See this feeling comes from deep in my core
And has never led me astray before

So i've chosen to be committed
With a love that's relentless
Passion so intensive
I'm ready to go the distance

The Passion Still Remains

We've said some hurtful things, but the passion
still remains
We've played some dangerous games, but the
passion still
remains

Our thoughts are not always the same, but the
passion still
remains

I've called you by her name, but the passion still
remains
You gave my love away, but the passion still
remains
I said I'll see you another day, but the passion
still remains
You told me you couldn't stay, but the passion
still remains
I surely went astray, but the passion still remains
I got on my knees and prayed, because the
passion still
remains

I asked God to make away, because the passion
still remains

Asked you to forgive me for my mistakes,
because the passion
still remains

Told you to give me another break, because the
passion still
remains

You got my baby on the way, and the passion
still remains
Its hard to make it through my day, because the
passion still
remains

I just need you to be my babe, because the
passion still
remains

I promise I will behave, because the passion still
remains
This time I will fly straight, because the passion
still remains
I need you to share my fate, because the passion
still remains
Your doubts, I will alleviate , because the
passion stills remains
I ask God to Mediate, because the passion still
remains

Patient Love

You ever stared face to face, with an answered prayer?

Firmly fixed in place and she's not going anywhere, unless you're there

You have a choice then, to be grateful or ungrateful

She just confirmed my beliefs, so i choose to be thankful

Lord knows i'm thankful

I cant keep my eyes off you, cant keep my mind of you

I'm waiting for the day that I can say that I cant keep my hands off you

It's ok, because what we have is a patient love

Anticipation building

I get chills in my spine, from thoughts that run through my mind

Only thing between us is time

This is a Patient Love

Sometimes its anxious love

We persist inspite of difficulties

Shaytan! Although he tries, its hard to taint this love

You fit me like a glove

Our trust is water tight

And you know wrong from right

I’m right in front of you, your patient lover

Waiting to lead you to paradise

Taking you as my wife

A quilt to comfort me

I’m all in you like my favorite pair of jeans

I’m all on you like your favorite pair of jeans

Save room for me

It aint no pairs of me

I’ve been waiting for some time now, so be prepared for me

Because i’ve been patient love

There’s alot of love to give

Alot of hugs and kisses

Need you to rub this tension

Its 4th quarter 4th down and inches

About to score ready to go the distance

Give you what you’ve been missing

I’ll be home soon

Until then, just continue to be patient love

Regrets

How can I want of you perfection, when my
own actions are
defective

There's no way I deserve to be respected
When I had one job with your heart, and failed
to protect it
How can I treat our love like an elective

When you have the option to be selective
Not to mention, I left you neglected
How can I be mad when you do what's expected
I showed you the door, I didn't think you would
exit
And just that fast, you're gone, ejected
Should of saw it coming, but I wasn't receptive
Knew my ways wasn't right, thought I had time
to correct it
I mishandled the jewel that I was blessed with
Left my heart broken and disconnected

So Sick

So sick of that lifestyle
Thankful that I got sat down, to appreciate my life and what's worth while
Its sad that sometimes it takes trials, for me to appreciate every minute in the hour
Just need a second or an instant
On the road to repentance
I'm ready to go the distance
To pray for some forgiveness
Do what it takes to fix this
Looking for the piece that's missing
Time for new beginnings
Need to try something different
Look at the life I was choosing
I was losing, time for improvement
Never cared how I was moving, or who I was using
Using women for amusement
Straight abusive
Her feelings useless
Came into their lives like intrusion
Left them in a state of confusion
Emotional bruising
On to the next, I was cruising

The Only Love I know

My love is magnetic
Its flowing in your direction
I give and receive with no interceptions
I crave what you bring to me
You're my obsession
I testify to our love, more than a confession
I feel no guilt, nor doubt, and I'm not stressing
I'll make your your love come down
In the natural way things flow
I'll make the excitement sprout
In the natural way things grow
I'm used to having my way
Not used to taking things slow
You may have to forgive me
Because that's the only love I know
I want to grow, I want to build
So i need you to help me yield
Whatever ails me and all my ills
Convert my negatives into skills
I know that I'm too passive
Help me to be pro active
May need a lesson in aggression
Or atleast change my perception
Either way it go
Be patient with me
Because that's the only love I know

Thoughts Run Free

Pen on paper letting my thoughts run free
Thinking about my life, and what's become of
me
All so many feelings, too long for summary
But still I search for words to give you some of
me
Right now I'm without my drug, I'm in recovery
Had to search within my soul for the discovery
Our little talks on the phone is not enough for
me
Not being able to hold you at night, Its tough to
sleep
Although I look forward to my dreams, to
refresh my memory
I stay up all night long remembering
Still feel the warmth of your body simmering

US

Our love is the lyrics to my favorite song, each
kiss is sweeter
than the first time

Our sex is like my favorite movie, and when it's
done I just
press rewind
Your touch is my favorite outfit, I throw you on
when it's cold
outside

Your tongue is my favorite snack, I need my fix,
I want you all
the time

Your stare is flammable, your smile still gives
me butterflies
Your laughter my favorite tune, your presence
fulfills my
appetite
Your beauty motivates me, enough to keep me
on my grind
Our trust is my favorite keepsake, I find it hard
to keep you off
my mind

You're Good

You talk a good game, love how you make your words dance

As I watch your lips move, you have me stuck in a trance

I can’t help but submit whenever I steal a glance

Lust elevated, and I know, I don't stand a chance

The type of girl we go out, I don't mind holding hands

I put my feelings on lock down, but my heart has other plans

I aint fishing for love, but this feel like romance

I’m ready to fulfill your needs, supply your demands

I know I’m high off new love, but I’m not ready to land

www.ingramcontent.com/pod-product-compliance
Lightning Source LLC
Chambersburg PA
CBHW051747130826
49812CB00033B/1041
9789357213875